Life, Love, Lessons, Feelings, and *More*

Brandon Butler

PAGE PUBLISHING
Conneaut Lake, PA

First originally published by Page Publishing 2024

ISBN 979-8-89315-942-4 (pbk)
ISBN 979-8-89315-959-2 (digital)

Right or Wrong

Right or wrong I stand up
For what I believe
Even If it's me against the world
If wrong God will judge me
But if right send me above

So Beautiful

So Beautiful
At the sight of you I fall for you
So Beautiful
Every day is a blessing to see you
So Beautiful
That no one can out shine you
You stand out like the brightest star
So Beautiful
I need more than words to explain
how Beautiful you are
So till then I'll just say you are So Beautiful

No Pain, No Understanding

To have never felt pain
Is to have no understanding
To have felt pain
Is to understand how it feels
To feel pain
Pain comes in many ways
What may not hurt you
May hurt another
But to overcome pain
Will make you stronger
So to have never felt pain
Is to have no understanding

Wonders

Night, night bedtime
Wake up - lights on
Turquoise - Ice on
Heartbreak - cold grill
Life splits - two lives
Down the river too dark
Seek to find - but lost in sight
Blind and calls out to eyes
Money a pair
Class the clown – Double Dare
The fear is near- Peek-A-Boo
Get a clue
And lace your shoe
Wondering thoughts – Wondering minds
I think about you all the time
In this life and next
I seek to find
The wonders of the world

I Know I Will

I know I will
Chase the dream like a needle in a haystack
Ray Charles – Blindfold
I can feel the dream
No doubt – I shine
Like diamonds in water
Thirst quencher – Gatorade
Powered in spirit
Flow like dust in the wind
Disappear like butterfly kisses
I Know I Will
Talent in mind, body, soul, and spirit
Caught tears in my eyes
Felt a glimpse of pain
Heart cold – Zero degrees
I Know I Will
I can – I believe
I'm the entertainment – I'm the show

Zoom out like a telescope
The future is bright
I say- Give me a chance

Fade Away

Fade away in to the dark
Peek-A-Boo found light
Grew wings - I could be your angel
Lost Heart – Found Spirit
Lost and Found
Grew up to Fairytales
Got a reality check
Seeking paper like heat seeking missiles
Remember me like planets in the sky
Everyone knows my name
Play like kids – Shadow is my friend
Fade Away
Only to be reminded of the light
Peace

Night

The nights of night
The world's biggest deepest dark fright
Night of the rain
Lies sorrows of pain
But at night in the end
Find comfort in the rain
And sleep till morning to wake up
To a brand new morning
Only to end another night

My Dream

To wake to a world of understanding
No longer being misunderstood
But knowing why people react
From where they came
To who they are
To let be left in the past
And look towards the present
To the Future
To let the understood be understood
And the misunderstood
What a Dream
Is my Dream

The Dream

To all the love
To all the pain
To the past, present, future
I'm here still standing
To all the failures
To all the accomplishments
I still believe my future is music
No one can change my mind
It's my love passion
And it burns in my blood
Like hell himself likes my music
Believe what you want
Believe whatever
But if you from the bottom
Then you know how it feels to have a Dream
An I'm chase mine to the Death of me
And when I die party and cry
And scream to the Heavens
But why I'm alive show me now

Puzzle

Run away from love
The love in the air
Do you dare to breathe?
Cross over to the other side
Can you see the future?
Lost in the world
Find the piece to the puzzle
Drama in the air
Time to relocate
New Life – New Wife – New Dreams
Closed eyes – Sleeping Beauty
Found piece
Sleeping beauty kissing puzzle piece

Walking Journey

The walk – The journey
Heart attaches – Feelings caught
The beauty in the air
Gorgeous Flower
To search – To find
The day – The night
Time together is full of fun
Never a waste
Found puzzle piece
You found the Key – Unlock
Time passes but your always on my mind
The end – Message sent – Complete
Forever together
One life – One puzzle

Dear Darling

I wake – I bake
I cook – I clean
For you my Darling – I'll do anything
For you are my child
I guard you with my Life
I shall do my best to raise you
And help you through trouble
For you are my prince or princess
Mommy spoils you the best
I wake – I bake
I cook – I Clean
For you my Darling – I'll do anything

Might

Just might make you wifey
As long as you stand by me
Just might go out the country
To get a taste of Italy
Just might fall in love
And comeback with a broken heart
Just might disappear
Lost in a maze
It's been days – It's been nights
Halloween fright night
Looking forward towards the future
Better days – Better nights
I sleep – No problem
In time I'll see
Till then I'm blind
Peace

Untold Cupid

Wonderful woman with outstanding features
Shine as bright as the night sky
Heart in the heavens – Good little Angel
Kiss in the night – catch butterflies
Music plays – No doubt
She glows like the morning sunrise
The feelings in the air are toxic
Deep breath – Love suffocation
Feel like a Fairytale love story
Make a wish -Shooting star
Make a wish – Candles
These days love fades
Like a bottle caught in a wave
Close my eyes – My imagination is clear
Deep thoughts – Deep minds
Closed blinds – Good night

Random Thoughts

The day seems long
The night goes slow
Together time is not a waste
To enjoy quality time – I wish upon a star
Your beauty sparkles in the night sky
Together cozy in bed
Feelings boil like overcooked hotdogs
To burst but not starburst
To merge and connect
To understand but not misunderstood
I seek – You seek
A game of Peek-A-Boo
To be found – By luck? Or destiny?
Like becomes – Like – Like
And builds on to something stronger
Called L-O-V-E
I seek – You seek – Peek-A-Boo

Special

Thy voice is like a cold breeze
I get goose bumps all the time
You shine, your bright
You're my Light
A day without you should be a crime
For thy eyes have never seen more beauty
Till this night
For you are a sparkle of a tear in the eye
Of Joy
Once seen, I never want to walk away
For your beauty has taken more hearts
Than Cupid has found Couples Love
For you are Cupid's lost loved
And the World can see
Why he's scarred
For thy has never seen such amazing beauty
In one place
For my eyes are forever lost in the magic
Love at First Sight

Thoughts of Wonder

Let flow to let go
Wave after wave
To walk on water – Miracles
Thrill Seeker
Only to be disappointed
World spins
Only to wake to sunshine
To only be misunderstood
Wonders of the world
To only be found in time
Why listen? -Why wait? -Why go?
Questions in need of answers
But no reply
To close my eyes
Rest in peace – Never wake
Night-Night

All I Know

All I know is to follow my Heart
The path of happiness is in reach
There is so many things to be happy about
But yet there is still depression in the world
I search to find the one
I can call my own
Dear Lover Where are you?
Smiles lift the spirit like balloons in the air
I seek to find like ying to yang
My fairytale dream filled with hope and happiness
The sky is blue – The clouds are white
My Heart skips a beat
Every time I think of you
All I Know is to follow my Heart
Seek love like a heat Missile
Target on lock
I'm out here searching for the key
Who has the key to my Heart?

All I Know is to follow my Heart
The end is near – the search is far
I shall seek

Space

She hollers in the wind
I need space
She calls my name
I need space
The kids cry
I need space
The Doctor warns me
I need space
My thoughts – My mind
I need space
Sometimes I'm lost
So I need space
Give me space
Let me rest in peace
My space – My space
Sometimes I just need my space

Independent

My house -My car
My job – My money
Independent
My life – My choices
My decisions – My risk
Independent
My bills – My time
My religion – My goals
Independent
My dream – My skills
My talent – My relationships
Independent
I seek to be on top
I seek to be independent
I seek to be my own Boss
I will be Independent

Show Me

To love me
Is to know me
To know me
Is to love me
To care
Is to cry with me
To hold me
Is to never let go
Show me you care
Show me you love me
Show me the passion – The fire – The love
Show me comfort
Show me a Fairytale in reality
Show me love exist
Show me Romeo & Juliet
To love me
Is to know me

To know me
Is to love me
Do you know and Love Me?

Zone

The time goes by
My heart pumps blood
The summer breeze in the air
Life drops – Dead rise
Sky blue – rainfalls
I stop for a second
Smell the air
For a minute, Love was in the air
I start rolling on my own – Flintstones
What I felt ain't there no more
I must got life backwards
Life's a little twisted
So I use my imagination
Then I change the radio
To my favorite station
I forget all problems
I'm in my zone

The time goes by
I couldn't care less
Like I'm Lifeless

Let's

Let's fly
Let's go bye-bye
Let's play in the clouds
Let's watch the sunrise
Let's – Let's
Let's relax
Let's blow kisses at the sky
In time I die
But at the moment
Let me live my life
Alright-Alright
Let's – Let's
Let the wind blow in my hair
Let the rain touch my skin
Let the sun shine on me
Let's – Let's
Let's go play outside
Let's dream of everlasting Life
Let's dream of Love in the sky

Let's – Let's
Let's shine together
Forever & Ever and Ever

Unwordable

The way I love you is unwordable
The way I care for every piece of hair
The way you move is so smooth
The way I feel is unpredictable
I'll do anything to make you happy
Even then I'll do more
It took a while to find you
But now that I have
I can't let you go
My only hope is that you love me to
My only hope is to be with you
It's hard to find one that feels what you feel
Understanding-Passion-Comfort-Caring-Everlasting
Feelings are strong even in death
To die peaceful without stress
You will one day have to rest
But till then I'll love you so

Hoping we never fall apart
Even in the end
You'll always be close to my Heart

Not a Judge

For I am not a judge
Like court
But I do express my opinion
But I speak and say out of Love
Not to offend you
Or defend you
Just to help open the world to options
As in like choices
For I am not a judge
But for those who do judge
Why behind my back?
And not in front
For I am not a judge
But we all have opinions
So express freely
For I am not a judge
But be respectful when judging

For I am not a judge
As I say
I am not a judge

Time

Water flows time passes
Understanding is at your reach
People come and go
No one here's to stay
The world is a mystery
So come out to play
To solve is to discover
To discover is to find
Why not try to have fun sometime
You can rest when your dead
So live life to the fullest
I'll ask again
Why not try to have fun sometime?

My Prayer

Hey God, How you doing?
I know you been watching
I been trying to hold up
I know I been struggling
So Thanks- For the drink in the cup
An food on the table
I know you help made me to the man
I am today
Cause no matter what came my way
Something good came out of it
It may have not been a lot
But it was enough
An that's all I can ask for
So Thank You
Amen

Mystery

The world is a mystery
People are a mystery
For the eyes show many things
But still they are a mystery
Why we do? What we do?
How we feel and How we make decisions
Is a mystery
Till the day we die we will never know all things
So let it be known there are many things to discover
In this world of mystery

The Day

The Day will come when you will shine
The Day will come when you'll understand
The Day will come-like a season and you will bloom
Like a flower
The Day will come when you feel
like you can't take no more
The Day will come to stand above others
The Day will come when it will rain
The Day will come when days
will never be the same
The Day will come when you will sleep
And never Awake
Sorry to say the day will come
But the day has yet to be known

Strength

Through all life struggles
I still stand
Through all the pain
I still have a Heart
For once I was in the dark
But found light- through a spark
I once was lost
But found meaning in life
To live through all the ups and downs
I stand today
To take life's challenge head on
And Live a Life
I'm Proud Of

Inspire

Up-Down-Circles
Inspire one – Overcome a Nation
Thoughts - light switches
From sticks to bricks
Sunrise to night sky
Never thought I see the day
Times update – Times change
Surf the wave – Flows of time
Never thought – But we did
So much change – From beginning to the end
Still pending
Always up for change
Never thought – We see these days
One world – Many drums
Let the music play
Many thoughts – Many minds
Inspire one – Overcome a Nation

Heart Sound

The Heart speaks
It wants what it wants
And need what it needs
Don't be silent
Let the Heart speak
To hold the truth
Is to one day to come out in light
So let the Heart shine bright
And say what must be said
Before the lies get to tall
And the truth weighs too much to bare
So let loose before it builds to high
Let the Heart speak
So it can rest in peace with no regrets
That's the best

Seek All

As I work
I seek to accomplish
No matter how bigger the wall
I shall give it my all
Till the day we all must fall
But till then I shall live a good life
Day by day saying thank you God
For waking me up this morning
No Matter how much it hurts
I shall give it my all
By the end of the day
I can take pride
Because I gave it all my effort

Helping Hand

I run fast
But time still goes the same
I surpass obstacles but no reward
For I am a giver
I pass Knowledge to the young
And inspect nothing in return
I Inspire like fire
Helping people rise to the occasion
For those who seek for help
Help shall be waiting for them
Where-When-Who
A helping hand shall wait
When in trouble you call to
The one and only God
This is the power of giving
To help a little
So, they might be able to change their lives
One Day

Dreams

The wind blows
The grass grows
Full moon light glows
The world is not the same
Players playing games
Real is dying out
Tears fall from the sky
No one recognize
An all I want do
Is fly away

Learn

The days go by
The nights come
The rain falls
Take it slow days – On the highway
One way – Not enough
I like options
And the choices that I make
Good or Bad
I learn from
Past – Let go
Present – Do right
Make that Future – Look bright
I'm doing – Alright

Once Was

There once was a boy
Whom walk with music in his ears
From dusk till dawn
He listened all day and night to music
For he knew every song and beat
But could not dance
People would watch and stare
As he shook his head
For his dream was to be
A DJ or Artist
As time went on he began to write
He had stacks of paper everywhere
From lyrics to chorus
An as time went on he began
To follow his dream
From early morning to night
He would go to the studio
People began to wonder as they saw him less and less
As days went by

Once he finished recording – It was time to perform
So he set a date and practice and practice
Then the day came and he was prepared
Lights flash cameras were on target
For it was time to see
IF he was ready
The lights flashed and cameras rolled
For it was time to shine
The day started slow but the night was a bang
Till this day he is proud
Till this day he shines like a star
For now his dream was coming true
To chase your dream is to Believe
Till this day you shall succeed
But only time will tell

Vibes

Ups and downs we all have frowns
Even the silent can make a sound
Sunrise I wake with a smile
Prepared to run every mile
End of the day
I must say
I think I changed someone's life today
Either good or bad
It is up to them
Neither easy or hard did I say it would be
But sometimes a change
Could be for the better
The Heart and the Brain are not the same
So listen to both
To help make choices
To wake-up one day
My eyes will open
I just help someone
Today

Bloom

This deeper than deep
Its space deep
I'm space minded
My eyes on the prize
The prize be the dream
The way I feel is like butterflies
Let me spread the magic
I can see the colors
But I don't judge the colors
Let it rain and let the sunlight shine
Let my Rose Bloom Brighter than the Stars

Karma

Wise man says
Comes around goes around – Karma chase
Love in the air
Do you dare breathe?
Fall on a cloud
Cozy pillows
Diamonds in the sky
Glisten like water in sunshine
Truth buried but still seeable
To seek but never see
To listen but not hear
To speak but not be heard
The mysteries of Life
To wonder but not forget
To remember is to be reminded
Look to discover
To only find – What you been looking for
Karma chase
Comes around-Goes around

Beyond Stars

Beautiful as you are
You are a beauty beyond stars
Your personality is relaxing
My mind set on goals
Together we shine
But you are my special ruby
The love in the air speaks
But all I hear is you
For I am your soldier
And I stand by you even in death
Forever like a guardian angel
May I rest by your side

A Heart Not Found

Mind gone
Heart Blown
Torn between two stones
Left one – Drop the other
Wondering where I should be?
Or where I could be?
My life is like destiny
But I forgot the address
Lost never to be found
Hearts bound in chains
The deeper dark
Is where cupid left his keys
So my Heart hasn't been release
That's why I'm not at peace

Older Is Better

The young can't vibe
The feeling of crimes
No pictures in the book
But still judged by the cover
I stay in the shadows
Only to be judged like Frankenstein
Never understood well
Till the pages have been read
I seek – I accomplish
I let go – I hide
The book adjusted to dust
To be picked by the unjudged
And read throughout history
Older is Better
For wisdom was given
Through Life Lessons

Attraction

Love is like a virus
You didn't ask for it
The Love just came
Feelings However can change
But even then
Love is still Love
For the Heart Feels
Yet some of us understand pain
For what is felt
Needs to be expressed
So flow with your Heart
Cause it can't speak by itself
So till then
Let It Flow

Could You Ever?

Could you ever Love a man like me?
A Man with Understanding
But not much of a talker
A man that will listen
But never try to be negative
A man who got your back
But understands when you want to be alone
A man who isn't going to look the other way
When you do wrong
But sometimes I break your Heart
A man that cares
But so confused on how to show you
I'm a man with its ups and downs
But still love my ladies
I'm a man with many Hearts
But I can learn on how to love one
Through all the ups and downs
Could you ever Love a man like me?

Heart

My heart was broke
My heart was lost
My heart was found
My heart was gone
My heart filled with passion
My heart burning in flames
My heart – My heart
Where is my heart?
My heart bleeds
My heart holds pain
Dear Heart
Where are you now?
My heart cold
My heart stops
My heart flows
My heart shattered
Dear Heart
Where did I leave you?
My heart was lost

My heart was gone
Dear Heart
Where have you gone?

Hope

The world will change one day
But not today
The world will be at peace
But not next week
I Hope for change
But where is the peace
I seek to be on top
Cause I started from the bottom
I rise like smoke clouds
Can you find the fire?
I'm burning with passion
I'll find Love one day
But till that day
I Hope the world change

If Only

If only I was younger
If only I was older
If only I was there
Our minds wonder
If only things could be different
If only I had said I Love You
If only you could understand
Our minds wonder
The world spins
Ideas drop
Life holds surprises
You can never really see it coming
If only
Our minds wonder
The never-ending wonder
If only
One day but not today

Will those questions ever be answered?
Till then
Our minds wonder

Times

There are times when I'm down
There are times to rise
The world spins – Time Flies
The kids play
Oh-What a Life?
What a Dream?
Was there ever a time of Love?
There are times when I'm down
There are times to rise
Life without meaning
Like a penny without a owner
I sure do miss those times
The Good – The Bad
The times we had
Oh-What a Life?
What a Dream?
Was there ever a time of Love?
The time – The time
The time Life, Dreams, and Love

Had Meaning
I Miss Times
Oh-Where are those times?

Love

What you seek is very deep and strong
The Power of becoming one
What you think is nothing
compared to how you feel
Your Heart Speaks for itself
Let's keep it real
Deal with trouble together never separate
Together you can surpass every obstacle
Even if you fail – You fall as one
Learn from your mistakes together
To take a step forward in life
What I speak of is real
If you can truly feel
What I speak of is True Love
Now tell me what you Feel?

Life
Love
Lessons
Feelings
And
More

SAVAGE

About the Author

Brandon Butler is a proud African American. He loves the magic of music and poetry and how it makes people feel. He has been writing poetry since the sixth grade. He had never thought of getting his poetry published, but now he's like, "Yeah, why not?"

He grew up mostly in Forest, Mississippi. He is what you would call an army brat (but his parents got divorced when he was young). Anyway, he has had his ups and downs in life. Music and poetry are how he speaks about his life.

He also likes William Shakespeare, like *Romeo and Juliet* (which he had read during high school class work). He hopes that his music and poetry will open doors for him and inspire people to become fans of his work.

His name is Brandon, also known as Bloom the Cancer, his artist name. (*Bloom* comes from his love of red roses, and *Cancer* is his zodiac sign.) Enjoy.

www.ingramcontent.com/pod-product-compliance
Lightning Source LLC
Chambersburg PA
CBHW021131130726
47988CB00003B/1259